Hildr Fragments

Dani L Smith

For Evelyn.

CONTENTS

CONTENT WARNING

Themes in this book include self-harm, abusive relationships, mental health, and miscarriage.

introduction

once upon a time there was a girl,

a romantic girl,

with her head in the clouds and a fanciful heart.

"la la land," her father said.

"you're not wordly aware."

the first knight came riding in,

a monkey on his banner.

rapist.

the second knight appeared,

a cowboy on his banner.

immature and naive.

the third knight swept her off her feet.

a bear on his banner.

her "true love"

…

abuser

drunk

liar

cheat

psychopath.

"la la land," her father said.

perhaps you are right.

yellow lions

stars and stripes

maple leaves:

you're all the same.

my life is full of fairy-tales

and abandonment.

my problem is that

everywhere i go

feels like home.

rb

i wasted four years

on a boy

who never told me

he loved me.

foolish girl.

always is always always.

"i'm pulling out.

it's not like you're enjoying it, anyway."

this is what you said.

as you raped me.

i remember the first time i cut in front of you,

the light in your eyes faded.

good, i thought,

leave me alone.

you said i didn't deserve anything,

that i should just

hurry up and kill myself.

i now know what i didn't deserve:

your bullshit.

how hard it is to lose mutual friends to a shallow rapist.

knowing that, if you ever opened your mouth, they'd never believe you.

a curious thing, the mind.

it can fool you into believing that nothing is wrong,

that these tears mean nothing,

that the urge to hurt yourself has no meaning.

it only fools you to protect you.

until the time is right, for you to process.

then one day,

when you're out of dangerous territory, and safe...

BOOM.

the memories hit you like a ton of bricks,

leave you gasping,

reaching for the drink,

crying in dark corners of nightclubs.

all the trauma, full force.

how could you have hidden this away? you demand of
yourself.

because now you're ready to heal, you reply.

jb

i met a cowboy once,

and he was the smartest of them all.

and darn, was he the cutest.

he could still have my heart,

if he asked for it.

i decided that i wanted you before even knowing your name.

what a complete turnaround

to go from talking everyday

and promises

to suddenly

"i'm done"

and ghosting.

"goodnight cowboy."

"sweet dreams, my english rose."

how ironic that the cowboy would become my biggest
cheerleader.

cowboy, you will never know how much your friendship and
endless messages have kept me going.

your weird love has kept me strong.

even if you disappear again and we stop talking for a while,

i know it won't be forever.

you're a constant, cowboy.

ddb

on our first date

you were 20 minutes late.

i should've known back then,

that you were trouble.

on our first date

you squeezed my elbow.

it was like a jolt of electricity,

every nerve lit up,

every cell was aflame.

i knew in that moment,

that no matter how it ended,

i wanted to go on an adventure with you.

the cards warned me about you,

but i didn't listen.

i sat on your ikea bed

and watched 6'3 of you

cook in your tiny kitchen

in your tiny apartment.

it had only been a month,

but i wanted to burst.

to tell you that i love you,

to scream it, yell it, sing it.

three weeks later,

you were the one,

to whisper those words first.

in the shadows of your apartment,

multicolour fairy-lights aglow.

your tears mixing with mine.

"i want to tell you."

"i know, so do i."

"but not yet."

"no."

"don't tell me unless you mean it."

i told you not to tell me you loved me.

not unless you meant it.

you told me, anyway.

but you didn't mean it.

you were the chips to my ice cream.

when i thought you were feeling lonely

i used to send you white balls of energy and positivity

conjured in my hands.

you made everything else so insignificant.

you were the one that mattered.

i wanted to be with you forever.

love is not a safe place

one blue sapphire

nestled between

two white sapphires.

white gold.

"it's like we're engaged to be engaged."

stupid, **<u>stupid</u>** girl.

"you know i'm going to ask you, right?"

you never did.

you once asked me

who i love more:

you

or my cat.

you got pissed off

when i couldn't answer.

we broke up

after five months of dating.

after that,

you searched for me

in my favourite bars,

and called me every disgusting name,

so i slapped you.

then you spat in my face

and ripped my books.

a month later

i was foolish enough

to agree to be your girlfriend again.

i should've listened to my friends about you.

to my parents.

heck,

i should've listened to my cat.

i cast a spell to bring you back.

it worked

but it came at a price, years later

in the form of my own blood.

scratched into the wooden viewing point at tiffany falls in ancaster, canada:

DdB ♥ DLS

i remember that day,

watching you etch a permanent sign of our love

for mother nature to see.

i knew things were going south

when you were angry that i didn't fold your laundry.

sometimes i think you were allergic to life.

i gave up so much for you.

food

drinks

money

friends

jobs

apartments

mj

but you gave up nothing for me.

why do you ask for my opinion,

or what i'd like,

when after my response,

you tell me,

what i should wear

what i should eat

what i should like

what i should aim for

what i should do.

why?

you never respected

my clothes

my friends

my family

my cat

my life

how could i have expected you to respect our relationship?

i had to sit down

and listen to and discuss

every criticism you had of me.

but if i deigned to criticise you,

you would ruin the entire day,

lash out in anger,

drink yourself into a stupor,

or sulk for three days.

human

i'm so used to the norm that is your drunken abuse,

that it unsettles me and fills me with anxiety when,

once in a blue moon,

you act civil.

it got to the point where

"i promise"

was like the kiss of death.

"i promise"

meant

you were definitely

going

to

break

it.

you

never

kept

a

single

promise

you <u>did</u> care about me

didn't you?

you <u>were</u> devoted to me

weren't you?

you <u>did</u> love me

didn't you?

even when i caught you in a lie

you somehow succeeded

in making me second-guess myself

and making me feel crazy.

tell me.

at what point did you decide

that you didn't

love me enough

to stay loyal?

i saw your searches

about emotional affairs.

i saw your screenshots

of her in lingerie.

her tits.

your lustful, drunken, stupid expression.

images burned in my brain.

i love you

please don't leave me.

사랑해

제발 날 떠나지 마세요.

ik hou van je
verlaat me alsjeblieft niet.

saya sayang awak
tolong jangan tinggalkan saya.

ti amo
per favore non lasciarmi.

わたしは、あなたを愛しています
どうか私を置いていかないでください。

ik hâld fan dy
graach net ferlitte my.

on my 28th birthday

you called me a glorious goddess

and told me that you needed me by your side.

your player two.

less than four weeks later

you were seeking her out.

"i'm *so* devoted to you."

is what you told me,

as you slunk away

to talk to

her.

i could taste the lies on your lips.

i wonder,

who she is,

this person who has been the other woman for you before.

more than a decade ago.

this person who can't even take you whole.

i wonder.

i don't get it.

her name is like a stain.

on my mind.

brain.

body.

soul.

how lucky she is,

that she never learned mine.

i have many names for her.

bitch.

cunt.

whore.

homewrecker.

thief.

desperate.

buck-toothed piece of shit.

she is all of these things.

but ultimately,

her true name:

betrayer of the sisterhood.

you told me that i was your unicorn,

but you chose a mule over me.

you said she is calm and sweet.

if that's what you want,

then i am wrong for you.

i made you a priority

but i was only your option.

homewrecker.

it is used for the other woman.

but you were the one that strayed.

you invited her in.

you lied.

you deceived.

it is you, who is the homewrecker.

how could you?

intimacy after infidelity.

they call it hysterical bonding.

reclaiming territory.

just because you didn't fuck anyone,

doesn't mean it hurts less.

lazy.

pothead.

anger issues.

entitlement.

zero sense of timeliness.

you, with your asian fetish,

and obsession with transsexual porn.

you, who objectifies all.

but you can't handle criticism.

you.

the typical white man.

you tell me not to yell,

as you yell at me.

you tell me not to talk over you,

as you talk over me.

you tell me not to interrupt,

as you interrupt me.

you tell me not to criticise,

as you criticise me.

you tell me not to vent,

as you vent at me.

i thought dating someone older

meant i'd be free of fuckboy drama.

what i got instead was a manchild,

emotionally stunted at 15.

your mouth,

contorted and twisted

in anger and foam,

always reminded me

of a butthole.

perfect,

for an asshole like you.

your parents didn't like you

from the day you were born.

their bouncing bundle of disappointment.

and yet,

they still enable your abusive ways.

you've never been held

accountable for your actions.

your mother thought you'd stolen some silver.

she asked me about it, but i hadn't seen anything.

i never believed you'd steal from your parents.

weeks later, you presented me with some silver

and said we could pawn it off in hard times.

you stole it, after all.

your poor parents.

they never deserved a son like you.

i gave up so much for you.

a job.

an apartment.

my cat.

friendships.

family.

my money.

what did you give up for me?

fuck all.

hey

do you remember

in malaysia

when you were mad

because i was eating a bag of crisps?

you were so pissed off

that you grabbed the bag

smashed it against the wall

and flushed it all down the toilet.

so i poured your alcohol down the sink

and you yanked me backwards

had me in a painful headlock

and tried to pour the rest of the alcohol on my head.

then you tried to break my bag

so i stomped on your foot.

the neighbours called security

and i had to pretend

that everything was fine.

and to this day

with all your dramatic flair

you claim i tried to break your foot

but in reality

you almost broke my neck.

do you remember?

"don't be a victim"

you said.

as you punched me.

one smack

two smacks

three smacks

four

five smacks

six smacks

seven smacks

more.

your response to being caught cheating

was to slap me.

the audacity

that you thought you could assault me

and get away with it.

do you really think that me stating what you are,

a psychopath,

was worse than your three years of manipulation?

you are closed fist

whereas i am open palm.

your betrayal hurt more

than master li's.

everybody lies

delusion

tell me

how do you sleep at night?

do you not choke on the bile of your actions?

feel suffocated by your lies?

cripple yourself with the weight of your manipulation?

break yourself with the fists that broke me?

how do you live with yourself?

tell me.

you painted this pretty little image of yourself

and made me fall in love with the idea of you.

but actions speak louder than words

and you were nothing but a disappointment.

i pity you.

it must be difficult

to reach the middle of your life

and have nothing to show for it.

you didn't even want to know

our daughter's name.

… it's Evelyn.

Evelyn.

i'm not a mother,

but i am a mother.

a child-less mother.

half a mother,

cradling air.

i'm terrified

that the baby i lost

was my one chance

at motherhood.

i bled in fortinos

we stood in an aisle

and whispered to each other

i moved away

but you pulled me closer

your face, crumpling

we embraced

and held each other

as we mourned.

i stood before you,

as you sat on the bed.

"please kiss my stomach,"

i asked.

you lifted my shirt, kissed,

and spoke,

"hey little one,

we'd sure like for you

to stick around."

our child

sat rotting inside of me

because pot and porn

and video games

meant more to you

than my health

and her well-being.

it wasn't the technician asking me about bleeding,

or his odd look of doubt,

or the fact that he wouldn't let me see the screen.

it was your expression.

you were watching the screen.

you went from nerves and excitement,

to blank and unreadable.

it was then.

i knew.

"hey little one."

with hands on my stomach.

"please be okay.

please, please, please."

i whispered this on the clinic table.

deep down, knowing you

were already gone.

for my first scan

i was in another country

without insurance

so i paid out of pocket.

the technician knew what was happening

but he couldn't discuss it.

he called me back from the bloods lab

said he had to scan again

because he'd "lost the data."

he was more forceful the second time

it hurt and i ached.

deep down, i think he took pity on me

and detached the placenta.

when we found out

that i was going to

miscarry our baby,

you expected me to

sit with you

at your dealer's house,

make nice, and pretend

that nothing was wrong.

after the scan,

and we had an idea of what was happening,

you didn't concern yourself with

sitting down with me

comforting me

talking.

instead, we had to go and make nice with your dealer.

at his place,

i started to miscarry.

on that evening

at your dealer's house

my stomach ached

and i felt wet.

in the bathroom

i pulled down my jeans

and was met with blood.

it had soaked through my clothes

and ran down my legs.

i wiped clots away with tissue.

i was miscarrying.

in the living room,

i whispered to you

what was happening.

that we had to leave.

you said, "in a bit."

i sat and bled for another hour

before you finally fucking moved.

it is an odd feeling,

to feel so numb,

when you're looking down,

at underwear,

filled with blood clots,

the size of a tiny fist.

the evening i miscarried

there was a downpour.

the rain mirrored

my blood.

they tell you it's like a heavy period.

what they don't tell you is it's like childbirth.

all the pain and the pushing and the contracting and the effort

without the happy ending.

it's like giving birth to a ghost.

no one tells you the truth about miscarrying

not the doctors

not the internet

or people.

"heavy cramps," they say.

the truth is:

contractions

labour

pain

pushing.

all of that without the end result

of a baby.

i had a dream

telling me

that the baby would've been a girl,

healthy,

and perfect in my eyes.

sometimes,

i am relieved,

that our band-aid conception never breathed life.

because she was saved from having

a psychopath for a father.

then,

i am consumed with guilt.

i saw a baby with the bluest eyes and it stopped me dead in my tracks.

she would've had blue eyes as well.

i was left to deal

with what would've been

our baby's due date

all by myself.

A vision of Evelyn rounding a corner in the house and yelling "Mommy!" as she beckons me to go with her. She has a Canadian accent. Her hair is pulled back to keep the light brown curls off her face. She smiles at me with a mouth full of milk teeth.

Haunted by the daughter I never got to have.

i have an image of my daughter

blue eyes and wild waves

racing against the wind

up the steps of Ta Keo.

at the top

she wipes the Cambodian heat off of her brow

turns

flashes a smile

and waves at me

as i follow suit

relishing in her fearlessness.

baby bear,

with eyes so bright

and hair so fair.

my beacon of light.

you were so small

but you left the biggest

mark on my life

escape

vanilla

nellie's laundry detergent

borage moisturiser

goat's milk soap

ligo hot sauce

weed

onion powder

cloves

sandalwood

peppermint

coconut oil

vick's vaporub

cinnamon tealights

freesias

maybe if i put all of these scents together

i can create a

whisper

of who

you once were.

my whole world fell apart

and you stood there,

the catalyst,

the cause of it all,

smirking.

waiting.

you wanted me to drown.

you wanted me to die.

you were my favourite person in the entire fucking world.

how could you?

you wanted to keep me hidden and tucked away

like a bouncy ball nestled deep in your pocket.

one that you would never let bounce

or achieve its true purpose.

the day that i escaped,

i bounced far away

and flashed every colour in the spectrum.

i bounced back to my true self.

free

you didn't love me,

so i left and loved myself.

i think you realised

once and for all

that you couldn't contain me

and never would.

i think that's why you became so vicious in the end.

let's face it,

you never deserved me.

period.

you are the worst person i've ever known.

so i left,

because i deserve nothing but the best,

and the best is yet to come.

the last time i saw you

you thought i was moving out

somewhere in the city.

you had no idea that i was leaving the country.

it gave me strength

to know

that you had no idea

where in the world i was.

it shook your control over me.

i feel like i lost my vocabulary when i left you.

i didn't leave the country

because i was scared of you.

i left because i was scared of myself.

of going back to you.

i miss you.

보고 싶어요.

mi manchi.

ik mis je.

ik mis dy.

when it rains

or snows

do you think of me

and remember

how much i love it?

"it can't have always been that bad, for you to stay so long."

yes, i admit.

but with a master manipulator, how do i know if any of it was real?

i'm suspended in air unsure if i'm going to plummet or soar.

"you shouldn't let one prick ruin it all," mother said.

but mum,

for a while,

he was my everything.

i was the best sex of your life

and you were the best sex of mine.

what now?

i never deserved your pain

and you never deserved my pleasure.

you made me feel so alone and unlovable,

but the moment i put out the call for help,

it felt like the whole world came rushing in to get me away from you.

it strikes me

usually when i'm driving at night.

my hand flies to my mouth

to stifle the shrieks and sobs.

i have to navigate the road

with eyes blurred by tears.

this is how you left me.

stumbling in the dark.

a week after i escaped you

i was in someone else's bed

with him on top of me

inside of me

his soft lips hungry against my own

i needed his touch to cleanse me

his kiss to remove the marks you left

his hands to wipe away the ghost of you.

afterwards,

i felt nothing.

not glad, not sad,

but relieved i got it out of the way.

motivational interviewing

"i'm not worth it," i wrote.

"so you have nothing to offer a relationship?" my therapist asked.

"yes, i do," i protested.

"but you're not worth it, so you have nothing to offer."

"but i do."

"so you *are* worth it."

i smiled.

"yes."

my best friend doesn't do

tears

emotions

romance.

i like that about her.

she doesn't have the patience

for that nonsense.

she's all about

tough love

moving forward

persevering.

nothing that

a good drink

a good dance

pizza dvd-bang nights

self-reflection sundays in a jjimjilbang*

can't solve.

* a Korean bathhouse

on the bench

facing the church

is where i eat my lunch

fish and chips with mushy peas

the path winds uphill

curving between the trees

and around the stone wall

the air picks up

the trees rustle

my back is to the village

turned away from civilisation

alone and feeling at peace.

despite all the shit you put me through,

deep down,

i knew that i'd be fine.

11 drunken, psychotic messages within one hour.

that's how you try and get my attention.

you don't understand.

i want my things back

not you.

people told me to forget the stuff that i left behind.

that it would be easier for me to buy it all again.

but it's not the same.

i could never forgive myself for abandoning the baby's things
in his evil clutches.

you referred to yourself as

"persona non grata."

i think that's the only

honest thing you've ever said.

stop messaging me

stop contacting me

stop harassing me

stop existing.

thanks.

in the end

you became the biggest villain

of my life.

i'd prefer 100 nightmares

over one dream about you.

i really hoped that 2016

would take you with it.

november 14th, 2017

today is your 40th birthday

and what do you have to show for it?

nothing but years of abusing, manipulating, and cheating on women.

congratulations.

you're a 40-year-old asshole

with no accomplishments to speak of

except battery, adultery, manipulation, theft, addiction
issues...

need i go on?

try me.

i dare you.

i have an arsenal of weapons

for when you try to mess with me.

where you keep your stash of weed.

your dealer's info.

the jailbait porn on your phone.

an email to your parents, detailing the physical assaults.

a trail of your abuse.

don't come for me,

because the police will come for **YOU**.

as i stepped out into the night,

i suddenly realised

that i'd never see you again.

i froze.

the crunch of the pebbles stopped.

i swayed on the spot.

i looked up at the sky as i processed that thought.

the stars winked at me.

i took a deep breath and decided,

that i was okay with that.

i rounded the corner,

and finished taking out the trash.

i belonged to you.

now i belong to myself.

i guess i never really loved you.

it's impossible to love someone that never existed.

you tried to feed off of my light

and shroud me in your darkness.

now i'm a fucking spotlight

and you're stumbling in the shadows.

i want to kiss someone until the whole world around me disappears and all that is left of me is a shimmer in the night.

conclusion

i wish that i could travel back to a year ago

to that beaten, broken girl

trapped and suffocating in that tiny room he forced her into.

i wish i could tell her

that her world wasn't falling apart

that her misery would soon end.

i wish i could tell her

how proud i am of her strength and bravery

tell her all the amazing things

that would happen over the next year.

i'm tired of writing poems

about a boy who wasted my time.

Printed in Great Britain
by Amazon